Animal Neighbors
Rat

Stephen Savage

New York

Published in 2009 by The Rosen Publishing Group Inc.
29 East 21st Street, New York, NY 10010

First Edition

Commissioning Editor: Victoria Brooker
Produced by Nutshell Media
Editor: Polly Goodman
Designer: Tim Mayer
Illustrator: Jackie Harland

Library of Congress Cataloging-in-Publication Data

Savage, Stephen, 1965-
Rat / Stephen Savage. — 1st ed.
p. cm. — (Animal neighbors)
Includes index.
ISBN 978-1-4358-4991-4 (library binding)
ISBN 978-1-4042-4568-6 (paperback)
ISBN 978-1-4042-4580-8 (6-pack)
1. Rats—Juvenile literature. I. Title.
QL737.R666S38 2009
599.35'2—dc22
                                    2008005451

Picture acknowledgements
FLPA 11 (R. Bird), 19 (Terry Whittaker), 20 (R. P. Lawrence), 21 (Terry Whittaker); naturepl.com Title page
(Paul Hobson), 10 (David Tipling), 12 (Warwick Sloss), 24 (David Kjaer), 2 bottom (David Tipling); NHPA
Cover (Stephen Dalton), 8 (Daniel Heuclin), 13, 25 (Stephen Dalton), 28 top (Daniel Heuclin); Oxford
Scientific Films 6 (John Downer), 7 (Paul Berquist/AA), 9 (Robin Redfern), 14 (Irvine Cushing), 15 (Mark
Hamblin), 16–17 (John Downer), 22 (Robin Redfern), 23 (Tony Tilford), 26 (Michael Leach), 27 (Ian
West), 28 right (Robin Redfern), 28 left (Tony Tilford).

Manufactured in China

Contents

Meet the Rat 4

The Rat Family 6

Birth and Growing Up 8

Habitat 12

Food 18

Finding a Mate 22

Threats 24

Rat Life Cycle 28

Rat Clues 29

Glossary 30

Finding Out More and Web Sites 31

Index 32

Meet the Rat

Rats are agile, intelligent rodents. They have adapted to almost every habitat, from fields and forests, to deserts, towns, and cities. Rats are found almost everywhere in the world apart from the polar regions.

This book looks at the brown rat, one of the most widespread of all the rat species.

Ears

Rats have an excellent sense of hearing, which is their main sense for detecting danger. They can also hear the communication sounds made by other rats.

Eyes

Rats can see well up to about a yard away, but over longer distances their eyes can only sense movement.

Nose

Rats have an acute sense of smell, which is used for finding food. It is also used to detect scents that mark territory and to recognize other rats.

Teeth

Like all rodents, rats have sharp incisor teeth, which continue to grow throughout their lives. The teeth must be ground down by gnawing on hard objects to stop them from growing too long. Molars farther back grind up food before it is swallowed.

Whiskers

Whiskers are very sensitive to touch. They help the rat to find its way around in the dark.

Forefeet

The forefeet are smaller than the hind feet. They can be used when it runs and walks, and to hold food while it eats.

Fur

Rats have long, oily, waterproof fur, which helps protect them against the cold and the damp.

RAT FACTS

The brown rat's scientific name is *Rattus novegicus*, **from the Latin words** *novegicus* **meaning "Norwegian" and** *rattus* **meaning "rat."**

Other common names include Norwegian rat, wharf rat, common rat, water rat, sewer rat, and house rat.

Male rats are known as bucks, females as does, and young rats as pups. A group of rats is known as a mischief.

The brown rat's body measures about 11 in. (28 cm) long without the tail. The tail is almost as long as the body. Adult brown rats weigh 7–14 ounces (200–400 grams).

Tail

A rat's tail is long, scaly, and almost completely hairless. It is held up in the air for balance as it walks along narrow objects and when it swims.

◀ A brown rat.

Hind legs

The rat's hind legs are long and powerful. The hind feet are large for running and climbing. Each toe ends with a tiny claw.

▲ This shows the size of a rat compared to an adult human hand.

The Rat Family

Rats belong to the largest group of mammals, a group scientists call the "mouselike group of rodents." This group includes various species of rats, mice, voles, and hamsters. Members of the group are all mouse-shaped, but they can vary greatly in size. Many dig burrows, where they live in colonies.

▼ **This black rat in India is stealing some tea from a glass.**

BLACK DEATH

In medieval times, the black rat was responsible for spreading the bubonic plague (also called the black death). This disease killed thousands of people in Europe. Fleas infected with the plague bacteria passed the disease to rats through bites. The disease passed to other fleas that bit the infected rat. People bitten by an infected flea or a rat caught the disease.

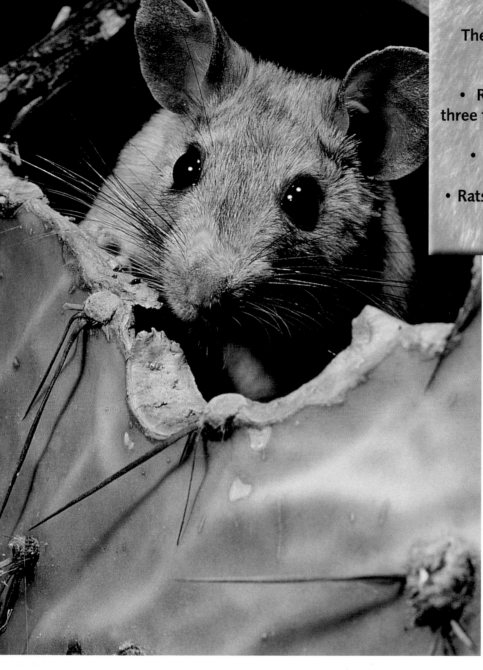

▲ Desert pack rats often build their nests in cacti. Apart from food, the cacti provide shelter from extreme desert temperatures and protection from predators.

Many rat species, such as the brown rat and the black rat, live near humans, often in or around homes, or near human activity.

Other types of rat live far away from humans and some are quite rare. The Australian stick-nest rat can only be found on a small island off the coast of Australia. It makes a strong nest from sticks up to 5 feet (1.5 meters) high. The desert pack rat lives in the deserts of North and Central America. It feeds on seeds, cactus, and other plants. Cactus plants are also a good source of water in this rat's desert habitat.

Birth and Growing Up

Rats can be born at any time of year, although most are born in the spring or fall. Before she gives birth, a pregnant doe makes a loose, round nest from dried grass and straw. She builds it in a chamber underground, where she will be safe from the prying eyes of predators.

RAT PUPS

Newborn pups are about 1.6 in. (4 cm) long and weigh about $^1/_5$–$^1/_4$ ounce (5–7 grams).

The average-sized litter is seven pups, although larger does can give birth to up to thirteen.

The newborn rat pups are pink, blind, and deaf, born with their eyes and ears tightly closed and with no fur. When they are about 3 days old, the pups may start to crawl, but they cannot move far.

A litter of six newborn pups huddle together in the nest for warmth.

▲ These 18-day-old pups jostle with each other as they drink their mother's milk.

The rat pups rely on their mother for food and protection. She cleans and suckles them several times a day and only leaves the nest to find food for herself. If the pups become distressed or cold, they make a high-pitched call to their mother.

Rat pups grow rapidly. By the time they are a week old, they are covered in a soft coat of fur and their eyes are open. Their teeth begin to grow when they are about 10 days old and they can hear from about 12 days old. The pups can now walk and begin to explore the nest chamber.

▲ These two young rats are exploring their surroundings.

COMMUNICATION

Many of the sounds that rats use to communicate with each other are too quiet for humans to hear. These quieter calls are messages to nearby rats, warning them of danger or calling for a lost pup. The calls only travel short distances, which prevents them from being heard by predators.

Early days

At 2 weeks old, the pups begin to leave the nest, following their mother as she looks for food. This is the time they get their first taste of solid food, copying their mother as she nibbles on seeds or waste food. Even though they have started to eat solid food, the doe continues to suckle her pups back at the nest.

Over the next week, the pups follow their mother on her foraging trips, learning the pathways that lead to food, escape routes, and dangerous areas to avoid in the area surrounding the nest.

At about 3 weeks old, the pups are completely weaned and eat just solid food. By now they may weigh more than 2.8 ounces (80 grams). They grow so quickly that their bodies do not grow in proportion. Young rats have large heads and feet compared with the rest of their body.

▼ Young rats can often be seen foraging on garbage heaps, where food is easy to find.

By the time they are 3 months old, the young rats have their adult fur and are fully grown. They may remain with the adult group, or travel to a new, unoccupied area.

Habitat

Rats can survive in many types of habitat, as long as they can find food, water, and shelter. Many live near people, taking advantage of their food and buildings. Rats are common in towns and large cities, where they are attracted by food waste.

Many rats live in or around houses, in warehouses, and around docks. Others live on garbage heaps and wasteland. Some rats are attracted to yards where people put out food for wild birds, or to places where pets are kept, tempted by their food and their bedding. Rats also live underground in sewer pipes, where they nest and find food.

▲ **Rats are very agile rodents, with powerful hind legs for leaping and climbing.**

SWIMMING

Rats are excellent swimmers and can hold their breath under water for four minutes. They can tread water and stay afloat for up to three days. Brown rats can swim against the water flow in sewage pipes, allowing them to move up and down the sewage system. They can even scamper through plumbing pipes and come up through toilets in disused houses.

In the countryside, rats live in barns, grain stores, and places where farm animals are kept. They often live near water, especially on riverbanks and around ponds. Since they are good swimmers, water provides an escape route from predators, as well as a source of food and fluids.

▼ Rats exit sewage systems at different places to find new sources of food.

The burrow

When they are not living in buildings or other
artificial structures, rats live underground. They live
in a burrow, a tunnel system that they dig
themselves. Rats use their front feet for digging soil,
which they push under their body and out behind
them with their hind feet.

The burrow is made up of several tunnels connected
together, and one or more chambers for nesting,
resting, and feeding. When a tunnel system is first
dug, it is only 12–20 in. (30–50 cm) long. However,
as a rat colony grows, more tunnels are added.

▲ A brown rat checks
for signs of danger
before leaving the
safety of its burrow.

Each burrow has one main entrance and many exits for a quick escape in times of danger. The entrance is usually dug in places where there is dense vegetation to hide beneath. This is often on sloping ground, such as a ditch or a riverbank. In a yard, the entrance may be against the wall of a house, on a rockery, or beneath a toolshed.

Territory and packs

Rats live in colonies called packs. A large pack can be made up of smaller groups called clans. Each clan or pack has a dominant male, and a group of does known as its harem. The dominant male is usually the biggest buck. He will mate with the largest does, which he accepts into his harem.

Each pack lives within its own territory, which is usually 16 ½–50 yards (15–45 m) around the central burrow. Rats mark the borders of their territory with urine, and with scent

MIGRATIONS

When there are too many rats living in one area, they sometimes carry out mass migrations. They swarm out into the streets looking for a new place to live with fewer rats. The German name for the brown rat is *wanderratte*, which means "roving rat," after these migrations.

▲ These rats have spilled out onto the streets in search of a new, less crowded place to live.

produced from special glands on the sides of their bodies. This is called scent-marking.

Rats have a group scent and can recognize other members of the pack through their smell. The bucks in each pack defend the territory from intruders, and fights can break out over territory borders and food.

Where there is plenty of food and shelter, territories are smaller because the rats do not need to travel far to get what they need. Large packs containing hundreds of rats can often be found around refuse dumps and sewers, where there is enough food and shelter to support many rats. In areas where food is scarce, territories are larger.

Food

Rats are omnivores, which means they eat both plants and animals. Their favorite food is grain. Rural rats feed on cereal crops, or cereal grain in grain stores. Urban rats feed on cookies, bread, and other foods made from grain, but they will also eat almost anything that humans eat. They are particularly attracted by food waste.

▼ **Brown rats are at the center of several food chains. (The illustrations are not to scale.)**

Rat food chain

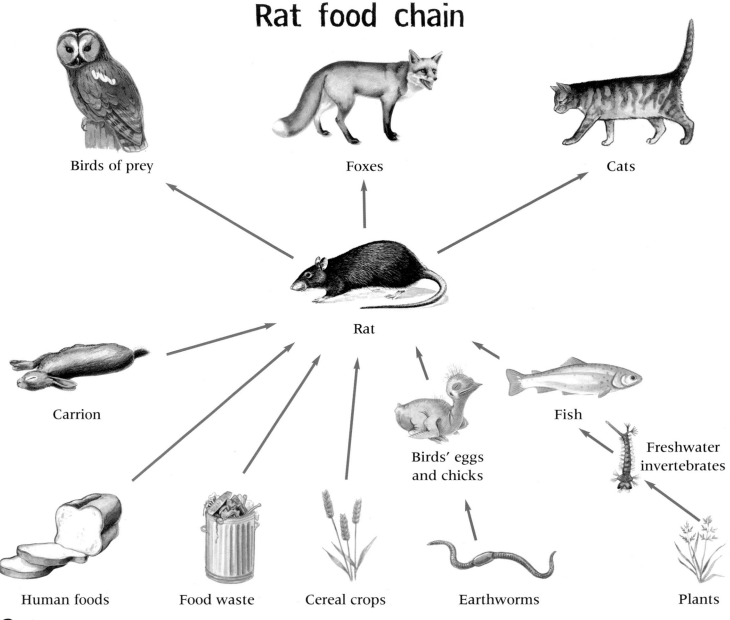

Birds of prey

Foxes

Cats

Rat

Carrion

Birds' eggs and chicks

Fish

Freshwater invertebrates

Human foods

Food waste

Cereal crops

Earthworms

Plants

▲ A hen will risk her own life to protect her eggs from predators such as rats.

Rats living near water catch fish and other small, aquatic creatures. They will also scavenge, eating the remains of dead animals, called carrion. Rats living near the coast feed on dead animals that are washed up on the shore at high tide.

Bird chicks and their eggs are another favorite food, especially those of ground-nesting birds, such as waterfowl and swans. The rat will usually try to steal the chicks or eggs from the nest while the parents are away, but sometimes they take them when the parents are present. Rats can kill chickens if they are cornered and cannot escape, and they occasionally kill and eat small mammals, such as mice.

Foraging

Since most of the rat's activity takes place at night, it relies on its sense of touch, using special body hairs and whiskers to find its way around in the dark. It also uses its excellent sense of smell to find food and avoid danger. Rats are particularly wary of any new scents they encounter. If a rat finds food out in the open, it will carry the food in its mouth to a safer place before eating.

Drinking water is very important for rats. In the countryside, they drink from ponds, streams, and puddles. Rats living in sewers beneath cities have a constant supply of water. In yards, they can drink from ponds and bird baths. Inside a house, they reach water from toilets and sinks. They even lick the water that has condensed on pipes.

▲ **Hanging upside-down, this rat is trying to get at the nuts in this bird feeder.**

▲ On farms, rats often eat grain that is meant for livestock, such as this hen feed.

Runs

Rats are very intelligent and memorize the various routes, or runs, in their territory. When it looks for food, the rat searches randomly at first. But once it has found a source of food, the rat will remember the shortest route to it, and use the run again and again.

Finding a Mate

When they reach a weight of about 4 ounces (115 grams), does are able to mate. This is usually after they are 11 weeks old. Young bucks cannot mate until they are older, because they grow slower in the company of a dominant male. This reduces the amount of breeding bucks in a pack at one time, which means there is less fighting.

▼ You can tell the difference between a doe and a buck because the buck (on the right below) is usually bigger.

BREEDING

Rats breed throughout most of the year.

The pups are born between 21 and 23 days after mating.

The average doe has four to seven litters of pups a year, successfully weaning 20 pups or more.

After the birth of her pups, the doe can mate again 18 hours later.

▶ This buck is finding out whether the doe is ready to mate.

Adult does are ready to mate every four or five days for about 20 hours. They will only mate with the dominant male in the pack. When a doe is ready, she gives the buck a signal by producing a special chemical from her body, called a pheromone. There is no courtship between the buck and the doe, and the buck leaves the doe to make a nest and rear her pups on her own.

23

Threats

Rats, especially young rats, have many predators. In the countryside, mammals, such as weasels and foxes, prey on rats. Birds of prey, such as hawks and owls, are also major predators. In towns and cities, cats and dogs prey on rats.

Younger rats can be prevented from reaching food at night by older and larger rats in the pack. They live on the edges of a pack and can be forced to look for food during the day, when they are an easy target for predators.

When food is scarce, rats can go without food for about two weeks. However, in such situations, rats may resort to cannibalism, eating the younger and weaker members of the pack. Does will fiercely defend their nest and young from attack by other rats.

► **The nocturnal European wildcat hunts mainly rabbits and rodents, including rats.**

24

Rats can live for up to 3 years in the wild, but few live beyond the age of 2 and most survive for only a year. Despite their short lifespan, rats produce so many litters of young a year, that rat populations in an area remain the same or may even increase.

▼ Rats have excellent hearing to detect predators, but barn owls swoop down on their prey in silence and take them by surprise.

People and rats

The brown rat's biggest threat is people. Rats have been killed as pests for thousands of years, but they still exist today in increasingly large numbers. On farms, they damage crops and stored grain. In buildings, they do a lot of damage gnawing wood, electricity cables, and even concrete and metal. Rats not only eat our foods, they contaminate it by nibbling or leaving droppings, making it unfit to eat.

CONTAMINATION

Rats contaminate three times the amount of food that they eat. They destroy more than $250 million of the world's stored and growing food each year, which would be enough to feed 200 million people.

▼ Rats eat and damage stored food. This rat has gotten into a box of potatoes.

The biggest reason why people kill rats is because they carry diseases that humans can catch. They can infect people's food with bacteria that causes food poisoning, which can make people very sick. They can also transmit Weil's disease through their urine. This bacteria can live in damp places and infect humans and domestic animals through cuts and grazes.

▶ Pet rats are slower and more docile than their wild relatives. If they are properly cared for, they do not pass diseases to their owners.

PET RATS

Rats have been specially bred as pets from wild brown rats, possibly since the mid-1800s. It is thought that this was done by breeding albino (white) rats with brown ones. Over many generations, this created a variety of colors including fawn, champagne, and lilac.

Rat Life Cycle

1 Newborn rat pups are blind, deaf, and furless. An average litter will have between six and eleven pups.

2 At 1 week old, the pups are covered in soft fur and their eyes are open. They can hear when they are 12 days old.

3 At about 2 weeks old, the pups follow their mother on feeding trips and start to eat solid food.

4 At about 3 weeks old, the pups are completely weaned and eat only solid food. Their mother may be pregnant again.

5 Does are ready to mate when they are about 11 weeks old. Bucks develop more slowly when a dominant male is present.

Rat Clues

Look for the following clues to help you find signs of a rat:

Burrow entrance
The entrance to a rat's burrow is usually a hole between 2.7–4.7 in. (70–120 mm) in diameter, made in grassy banks, under tree roots, or at the edge of sidewalks and drain cover areas.

Nest
A loose ball of plant material, paper, cloth, or other materials may be a sign that rats are nesting nearby. Nests can be found in attics and under floorboards.

Runs
Rats follow the same routes, or runs, through their territory every night. Outside, they may leave trails through grass and low vegetation. The trails look like walkways beneath the vegetation.

Gnawing marks
Look for signs of gnawing on nonfood materials. Teeth marks are small and usually appear lighter than the rest of the wood.

Droppings
Rat droppings are found along trails frequently used by rats. They are small, black, and cylindrical, and slightly tapered at both ends.

0.5 in. (12 mm)

Grease marks
Rats often leave rub marks against walls, pipes, and holes in buildings. These are greasy deposits left by the oils in the rats' fur.

Sounds
Rats make occasional squeaks or scuttling sounds as they run around behind a wall or in a loft. The most common sound of a rat is its gnawing.

Footprints
Rats have four toes on the fore foot and five toes on the hind foot. Prints may be seen in the dust in buildings or in the mud by a stream or pond.

Hind foot   Front foot

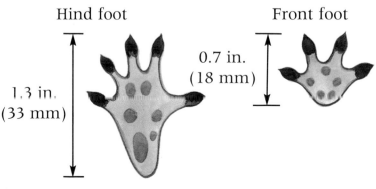

0.7 in. (18 mm)

1.3 in. (33 mm)

Glossary

aquatic Living in water, for example an animal that can live all or part of the time in water.

bacteria Microscopic creatures that live all around us. Some are useful, but others cause disease.

buck A male rat. The males of other species, such as deer, rabbits, and squirrels, are also called bucks.

carrion The body of a dead animal that is found and eaten by another animal.

cereal crops Crops such as wheat, barley, and corn, which produce grain that is used for food.

colony A group of the same type of animals that live together.

contaminate To make something impure by having contact with it.

doe A female rat. The females of other animal species, such as deer, rabbits, and squirrels, are also called does.

dominant The largest, strongest animal of the group.

foraging Searching for food.

habitat The area where an animal or plant naturally lives.

incisor teeth Sharp teeth at the front of the mouth used for biting or cutting.

litter A group of young animals born at the same time from the same mother.

molars Large, flat teeth at the back of the mouth used for chewing and grinding food.

omnivore An animal that eats all types of food, both animal and plants.

pack A group of rats that live together. Wolves also live in a pack.

predator An animal that kills and eats other animals.

prey Animals that are killed and eaten by predators.

pup A young rat. Young dogs, seals, and bats are also called pups.

rodents Small animals, such as rats, mice, and voles, with sharp, gnawing teeth.

rural A habitat in the countryside.

scavenge To eat the dead remains of other animals.

suckle When a mother allows her young to drink milk from her teats.

territory An area that an animal or group or animals defend against others of the same species.

urban A habitat in a town or city.

vegetation Various different plants that grow together forming a covering on the ground.

weaned A young mammal is weaned when it stops taking milk from its mother and eats only solid food.

Finding Out More

Other books to read

Animal Babies: Mammals by Rod Theodorou (Heinemann, 1999)

Animal Classification by Polly Goodman (Hodder Wayland, 2004)

Animal Sanctuary by John Bryant (Open Gate Press, 1999)

Classifying Living Things: Classifying Mammals by Andrew Solway (Heinemann, 2003)

Illustrated Encyclopedia of Animals: In Nature and Myth by Fran Pickering (Chrysalis, 2003)

Life Cycles: Cats and Other Mammals by Sally Morgan (Chrysalis, 2001)

Living Nature: Mammals by Angela Royston (Chrysalis, 2005)

My Pet: Rats and Mice by Honor Head (Raintree Steck-Vaughn, 2000)

Outside and Inside: Rats and Mice by Sandra Markle (Atheneum, 2001)

Science Around Us: Mammals by Peter Murray (Child's World, 2004)

Weird Wildlife: Mammals by Jen Green (Raintree Steck-Vaughn, 2003)

What's the Difference?: Mammals by Stephen Savage (Raintree Steck-Vaughn, 2000)

Web Sites

Due to the changing nature of Internet links, PowerKids Press has developed an online list of Web Sites related to the subject of this book. This site is updated regularly. Please use this link to access this list:
www.powerkidslinks.com/ani/rat

Index

Page numbers in **bold** refer to a photograph or illustration.

bacteria 6, 27

birth 8, 23, 28

breeding 23

burrows 6, **14**, 15, **29**

climbing 5

colonies 6, 14, 16

communication 9, 10

contamination 26

diet **18–19**

disease 6, 27

drinking **6**, 15, 20

droppings 26, **29**

feet **4**, **5**, 14

food 9, 10, **11**, **18–21**

footprints **29**

foraging 10, **11**, **20**

fur **5**, 8, **9**, 11, **28**

gnawing 4, 26, 29

habitats 4, 7, **12–17**

history 6

lifespan 25

litter **8**, **9**, 23, **28**

mice 7

migrations **16–17**

name 5

nest **7–9**, 10, **29**

pests 26

pets 12, **27**

pheromones 23

plague 6

predators 8, 10, **24**, **25**

prey **18**, **19**, **24–25**

rats

   black **6**, 7

   desert pack **7**

   stick-nest 7

running 4 ,5

runs 21, 29

scent-marking 17

shelter **7**, 12, 17

size **5**, 7, 8, 11

smell 4, 20

suckle **9**, 10

swimming 5, 7, 13

tail **5**, 7

teeth 4, 9

territory 4, 16–17, 21

urine 17

water 7, 12, **13**, **15**, 20

weight 8, 11, 22

whiskers **4**, 20